BOATING

OUTDOOR ADVENTURES

DAVID ARMENTROUT

The Rourke Press, Inc.
Vero Beach, Florida 32964

David Armentrout specializes in nonfiction writing and has had several book series published for primary schools. He resides in Cincinnati with his wife and two children.

PHOTO CREDITS
© Gordon Wiltsie: cover, page 7; © East Coast Studios: pages 4, 9, 16, 18, 19; © Chuck Mason/International Stock: pages 6, 12, 15; © Eric Sanford/International Stock: page 10; © Greg Johnston/International Stock: page 21; © Maratea/International Stock: page 22; © Panther Airboat: page 13

EDITORIAL SERVICES:
Penworthy Learning Systems

Library of Congress Cataloging-in-Publication Data

Armentrout, David, 1962-
     Boating / David Armentrout.
        p. cm. — (Outdoor adventures)
     Includes index.
     Summary: Examines various recreational uses of boats, including kayaking, canoeing, sailing, and whitewater rafting, and stresses the importance of water rules and safety.
     ISBN 1-57103-201-0
     1. Boats and boating—Juvenile literature. [1. Boats and boating.] I. Title II. Series: Armentrout, David. 1962- Outdoor adventures.
GV775.A75 1998
797.1—dc21   98–18413
                                                                          CIP
                                                                          AC

Printed in the USA

TABLE OF CONTENTS

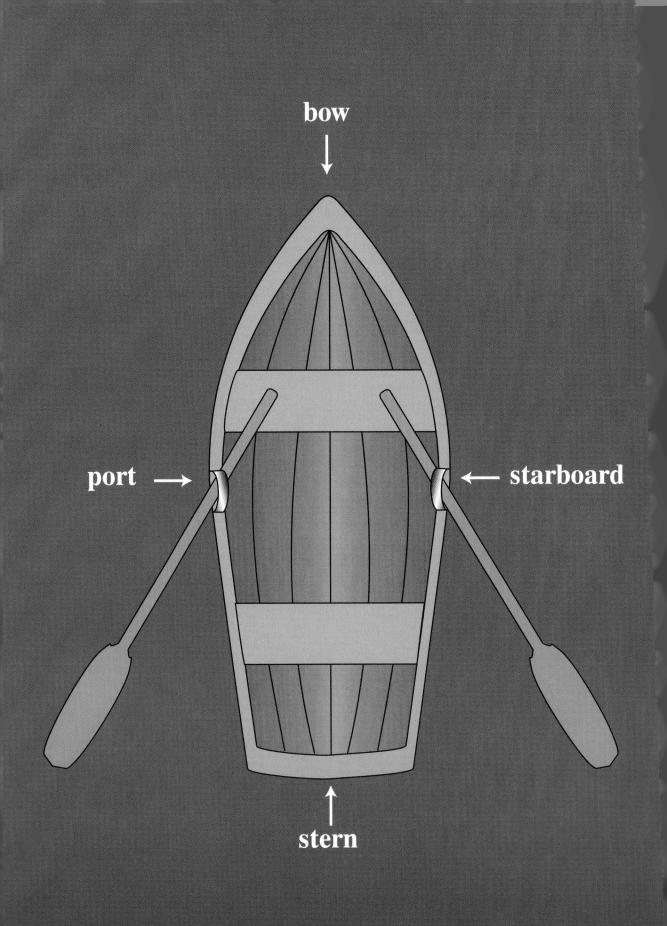

BOATS

Boats are used for many reasons. Fishing, racing, and rescue are just a few ways people use boats; but most people go boating just for the fun of it.

Boats come in many shapes and sizes. **Kayaks** (KY aks) are small and are made for one or two people. **Yachts** (YAHTS) are big boats that can carry several people. There are even houseboats that some people live on or stay on when vacationing on a lake or river.

All boats have a bow, or front, and a stern, or back. When you are on a boat and facing the bow, the left side is port; the right side is called starboard.

KAYAKING AND CANOEING

Kayaks and canoes are great for traveling on rivers. Kayaks are made to carry one or two people. A canoe can carry as many as four.

Paddles are used to move kayaks and canoes through water. The middle of a kayak paddle is the handle, and there is a flat blade on each end. Canoe paddles have a blade on one end and a handle on the other.

Kayaks come in many different sizes.

These boys use a canoe to find the best fishing spots.

A canoe livery is a place alongside a river that offers trips down the river. Canoe and kayak trips are great family and group activities. You can paddle at your own pace, stop for a picnic lunch along the riverbank, and even go for a swim.

SAILING

Sailboats use the power of wind to move through water. People have sailed around the world without stopping by using the power of wind. Only one sail is needed for a sailboat to move, but the more sails there are the faster the boat will go.

Sailing takes great skill. You have to learn how to raise, or **hoist** (hoyst), the sails and how to sail in the direction you want to go. If the wind is blowing the wrong way, driving you off course, a skill called tacking can be used. Tacking is driving the boat in a zig-zag direction so that the sails catch the power of the wind.

This sailboat has two sails to help catch the wind.

WHITE WATER RAFTING

White water rafting is a great way to explore mountain rivers and is fun for people who like adventure. White water is fast-moving water. Rafts often need to be directed around rocks, trees, and swirling water holes.

Rafts are made of **inflated** (in FLAYT ed) rubber and like canoes, they are moved with paddles. Usually a team of people paddle a raft together.

White water rafting can be challenging and rough at times, so rafters always wear helmets and life jackets.

White water rafting sometimes feels like a roller coaster on water.

POWERBOATS

Powerboats have an engine, or motor, and a **propeller** (pruh PEL er). The engine makes the propeller spin. The propeller spins in the water and makes the boat move. Engine-powered boats can move fast. Powerboats are seen on lakes, rivers, and the ocean. They are used for fishing, skiing, and cruising.

Powerboats are great for pulling skiers and "tubers."

This airboat is cruising across a lake.

An airboat is also a powerboat. It has a giant propeller. Instead of spinning in the water, an airboat's propeller is made to spin in the air. An airboat's propeller is always inside a steel cage for safety.

BOAT RACING

Boats are used for many activities. One fun activity is racing. There is a race for every type of boat.

Owners of small boats, like canoes and kayaks, often race on small lakes and rivers. Large powerboats race on big lakes and on the ocean. Some powerboats go over 200 miles (322 kilometers) an hour and need plenty of room.

Sailboat races, called **regattas** (ri GAH tuz), are very popular. Some sailors race their boats in small lakes, while others race around the world.

Powerboats race across the water at a very high speed.

COMPASS AND ANCHOR

When you are on a river, lake, or ocean, there are no road signs to help you find your way. A **compass** (KUM pus) next to the wheel can help you guide the boat. Boat captains travel the world safely with the help of a compass.

An **anchor** (ANG kur) is used to keep the boat from drifting when you have found a place to stop. It is attached to the boat with a rope or chain. When dropped overboard, it keeps the boat in place with its weight, or by catching on the sandy bottom.

Most powerboats use gauges similar to those in a car.

RULES OF THE WATER

Boaters must follow the rules of the water like car drivers must follow the rules of the road. Boating rules help keep the waters safe for everyone.

Following the rules of this sign may keep a boater from hurting a manatee.

The Marine Patrol and Coast Guard are the police on the water.

The best way to learn about boating is to take a safe boating course approved by the U.S. Coast Guard.

Boating courses teach basic boating skills, such as how to **navigate** (NAV eh GAYT) a boat, operate a radio, and avoid crashes.

SAFETY

Safety in and on the water is a must. You can stay safe and enjoy your time on the water by practicing these safety rules:

Always wear a life jacket when you are near deep or fast-moving water.

Watch for approaching bad weather. Don't get caught in a dangerous storm.

Carry a first-aid kit that includes sunscreen and insect repellent.

Be careful when handling fishing gear and fish, such as catfish, that have sharp spines.

Be aware of other boaters around you and follow all boating rules.

Most importantly, always let someone know where you will be boating and when you expect to return.

Boating is fun when done safely.

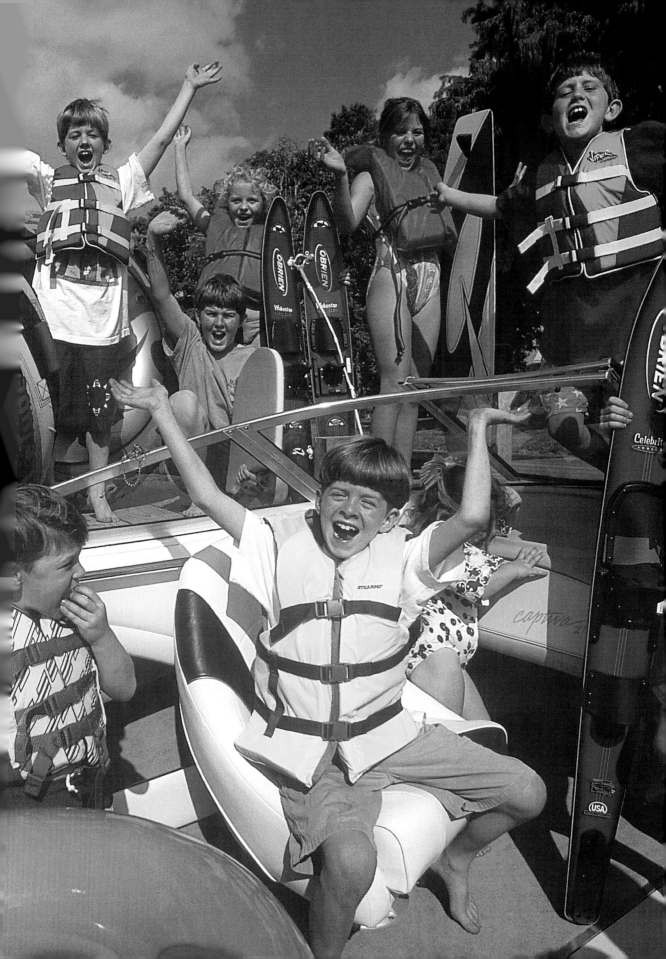

GLOSSARY

anchor (ANG kur) — a heavy metal object attached to a boat that can be thrown in the water to hold the boat in place

compass (KUM pus) — a device that shows direction

hoist (hoyst) — to raise or lift

kayak (KY ak) — a small, light boat, similar to a canoe, propelled by a double-blade paddle

inflated (in FLAYT ed) — blown up with air

navigate (NAV eh GAYT) — to steer or direct a course

propeller (pruh PEL er) — a device with rotating blades that causes movement, such as a boat propeller or an airplane propeller

regattas (ri GAH tuz) — rowing, speedboat, or sailing races

yacht (YAHT) — a big boat that can carry several people

This boy gets a chance to drive a large sailboat.

INDEX

FURTHER READING

Find out more about Outdoor Adventures with these helpful books:

Schryver, Doug. *Sailing School.* Barron's Woodbury, 1987.

Armstrong, Bob. *Getting Started in Powerboating.* International Marine Pub. Co., 1990.

Shears, Nick. *Paddle America—A Guide to Trips and Outfitters in All 50 States.* Starfish Press, 1992.

Hamiltion, Katie and Gene. *Practical Boating Skills.* Hearst Marine Books, 1995.